The
Presence

The Presence

POEMS 1984–87

KATHLEEN
RAINE

GOLGONOOZA
PRESS

In memory of
Hubert Howard

Grateful acknowledgement is
made to the following journals:
Acumen, Agenda, Chapman,
The Tablet, Temenos (London),
and *Words International*.

First published 1987 by
Golgonooza Press
3 Cambridge Drive
Ipswich, IP2 9EP, UK

Reprinted in paperback 1994

ISBN 0 903880 62 8

A catalogue record for this book
is available from the British Library

Typeset by Goodfellow & Egan, Cambridge
Printed at St Edmundsbury Press

CONTENTS

ह**

A Departure 9
In Paralda's Kingdom 16
Light Over Water 19
Mimosa-Spray 21
A Winter Night 22
A small matter 24
World's music changes 25
Tell me, dark world 26
I had meant to write a different poem 27
The Fore-Mother 28
Lily-of-the-Valley 29
The Presence 30
Threading my way, devious in its weaving 31
Woodruff 32
Say all is illusion 33
World, what have you done 34
Yes, it is present all, always—but these 35
That flash of joy 36
Change 37
Named 38
An Old Story 40
Blue Columbines 43
SEVEN SHORT POEMS
  Paradise—still I see 44
  In the November dawn 44

Paper-white narcissi   44
Again the scent of lime   44
Downpour from thunder-cloud   45
Flies—   45
The Western Path   45
A Reckoning   46
The untold! My life all   49
FIVE POEMS
Friends, who say   50
Can I give comfort?   50
Into what future do we pursue them   50
At last the awaited opportunity, time free   51
Hand, pen   51
Even now, sky   52
Christmas-Tree   53
Nataraja   54
Nameless Rose   56
What of life?   57
The Invisible Kingdom   58
Story's End   60
What human babe   61
Honesty   62
H.G.A.   63
A Dream   64
Hidden   65
Have I not heard   66
Jessie   67
Who Are We?   68

All Souls   69
A Candle for All Saints, All Souls   70
London Rain   72
London Wind   73
Words of Wisdom   74
Before my eyes this page, my writing hand   75
Joy   76
From a Guest-Room, in Fiesole   78
Purify   79

A DEPARTURE

I

ALWAYS and only in the present, the garden,
Always today of past and future the sum,

Endless everlasting light in flower
In flowers and leaves, in boundless sky pure.

East of the westering sun, west of the new moon
Stands my small northern house and daffodils in
        bloom,

Yet in this wide beautiful eternal place
My heart is sore with memories and loss,

For I am leaving you, my little world,
That still today shines with the golden light,

End and beginning of the one epiphany
Here and now of all that was, all that will be.

Grief, departure, exile—what are these
Mute Eumenides, who for all the bird-song and the
        daisies
Compel from my reluctant eyes these futile tears?

II

'Be glad' (a far voice speaks to me)
'Be glad you are required to part
'From all that withholds you from being free
'As the hills, as the clouds, as bird and tree.
'Break all bonds, old woman, while you may,
'Enter your own eternity.'

'Then what is grief?' I reply,
'Unriddle me this sore heart
'That has no words, but tells and tells
'From mother to daughter, daughter to mother
'That love must choose, over and over,
'Mortal things, all earth's minute
'Petals and wings.'

'You have loved other gardens long ago,
'And all in the one green veil are woven together,
'Unbroken the stream of the light, the stream of the
                air,
'Seed to grass, acorn to oak, forest to fire,
'The unborn and the dead companion you everywhere,
'Where you have been always, you are.'

'It is their transience makes dear
'Places and days that once were home,
'Sheltering refuges of earth
'Nearest at heart when they are gone,
'Faces we do not see again;
'Is it not death that seals our love?'

III

It winds into the heart,
That unbroken thread
From present to past,
Without to within,
From seen to seer,
Sky, garden, tree, bird
Transmuted, transposed
To memory, to pain
These young leaves, these daisies,
The dappling wind
That glances on blades

Of glistering grass,
Become what I am
Who am the sum
Of all I have lost,
Who am the maker,
From greenness a joy,
From wind, wisdom,
From cold earth, gold,
From gold of the sun
Life-blood of sorrow
That sounds the heart.
I am my past
And future approaching
Days unknown.

But of all these none
Brighter nor dearer
Than the wind and the daisies,
The little hedge-sparrow
Fearless and sun-glossed
Searching the flower-bed
Outside my window,
Winged with time
The ever-present
Flitting and flaunting
Its here and now
Light into love,
Leaf into loss.

IV

Vista of winter woods where we will go no more—
The frozen lake, mute swans; beyond,
That château all remember
Where dwells, or where once dwelt—

I glimpsed, long, long ago, the place, but they are
    dead to us
Who in another time, another land
Are what we might have been, might be
If world were reverie, or dream a world.

The two black watch-dogs guard;
Propitiatory cake to close those mouths—
Hope out of what memory
Like music in still air, as if—but here
The dream is changed: no door into that house.

                    v

Into this meagre earth, all these last years,
Imagined paradise has in these budding apple-trees,
These daisies closing in the evening grass,
Sent down invisible roots
That now I must tear up again,
From this little house wrench its inhabiting dream.

This quiet room—
Oak cupboard, lamp, the jug of daffodils,
The little bunch of wood anemones
Left by my granddaughter who herself is gone,
This sheltering present only another memory-place
Where loved ghosts wander,
Who are ourselves grown tenuous
Haunters of home we can never re-enter.

My mother's arm-chair, the writing-desk where my
    father
Kept faded snapshots, his sister's bible, my
    grandfather's last letter;
Painting of a rainbow a friend made from this very
    window,

The cups and plates, the dominos and jigsaw-puzzles,
The cat hearth-rug and faded Morris curtains
Never again together.
Moss and sticks do not make a nest, but the careful
        weaver
Of fragments the winter winds will scatter.

Logs glow on the hearth, the evening sky is clear
In the west where the sun has set, darker
Where the rising moon, one day past Easter,
Is veiled in cloud. Snipe whirr
Over the marsh: it seems that never
Could I let go this here and now;
But on my unsteady table yet again I write in sorrow:

Eternity's long now is for us unending departure.

VI

This, my last home
Is woven of memories
Lifelong; my mother's
Bridal-gifts, linen
Her fingers sewed,
Her work-table stored
With thimble and skein.
I have lived on
In my mother's world
With things her fingers
Endeared by touch,
Cake-tins, kitchen gear
Tell of her life,
Of hearth and table
Swept and spread
For husband and child,
Silent messengers

Charged with her love
To be delivered
Now she is gone
Who from her dreams
Drew out each clue
To be unwound,
Each stitch a thought
To clothe, to hold fast
Her one daughter
Someday in a future
That is now my past.

It is myself
I leave behind,
My mother's child,
Simple, unlearned,
Whose soul's country
Was these bright hills,
This northern sky.

VII

Take but a step
And there is no return,
Look back from the field gate,
Home is already gone.

'I could have changed my mind'—
But the one mind knows all
Future and past together
In the unchanging whole.

'What if some other way
'The price were found
'I need to keep this house,
'Could I not then stay?

14 ॐ

'What is the sum I need
'But loaves and fishes multiplied?'
But even he
Whose hands bestowed

Harvest of earth and sea
Knew when his time had come,
Might not evade
By the mere turning of an ass's head

What he had to do,
Although he chose
Of all the directions of the world
The worst road.

VIII

What, then, do they gain
Who follow an invisible master,
Leave home, wife, father and mother?
Nothing! Who can bargain
With that giver who takes all?
But being what we are, must travel;
Who are ourselves his way unknown,
His untold truth, his light unseen.

IN PARALDA'S KINGDOM

I

ALL day I have listened to their voices sounding
Over the high fells, the wind's kingdom,
Unhindered elementals of the air,
Their long continuous word meaning
Neither sorrow nor joy, loud singing
Great angels of the stars will hear when I am gone.

II

At rest in changing:
Across the blue they move
Passive in the embrace of the winds of heaven,
Visible melting into invisible, to reappear
In wisp and fringe of pure
Vapour of whitest mist as slowly they gather and
    come together
In serene for ever
Unbroken comingling consummation of water and air.

III

They accuse none,
Rays of the westering sun, or these
Folding clover leaves and sleeping daisies,
The missel-thrush that sings
To me, to all within the compass of his song,
My neighbour field-mouse
Venturing tremulous from hide under stone
Accepts the crumbs I have scattered;
From grass-blade to farthest star nothing withheld

From the unjust or the just; whom also made
The giver of these.

IV

Swift cloud streaming over the northern hill,
One moment dark, then vanishing
To rise in pulsing multitude
Of wings, turning again, returning, pouring
In current of invisible wind, condensing
In black core, to burst again
In smoke of flight windborne, upborne
Dust moved by will
Of single soul in joy innumerable, and I
The watcher rise with the rising, pour with the
        descending
Cloud of the living, read in the evening sky
The unending word they spell, delight.

V

Long ago, over the Northumbrian moors, as I lay safe
        in bed
I heard the elemental host
On chariot clouds riding the wings of the wind.
Framed text on my bedroom wall in daylight read
'Children obey your parents in the Lord,
'For this is right'; but in the outer night
Unborn undying voices instructed me:
'You were with us before you entered that warm womb,
'Free as we are free; none tells
'The wind how it should blow, the stars their courses.'
                                        And I,

A child remembering that anterior state

Communed with them; and still I hear them
Uttering a wisdom I have lost over the bare hills.

VI

Stillness after storm, heart at rest
In quiet song
Of missel-thrush; the winds
Have fallen, their work done.

I who am of another kingdom
Yet have endured their blast,
Attended their wisdom,
My work too ended,

Who to their wild voices
Have added my descant
Of joy and sorrow,
Sounding of intangible thought.

Who made that music
Alone can know
What meaning moves
When gale winds from the hills blow.

VII

On wet west wind soft sift of rain
Wafts from birch and briar breath
Of invisible life on the invisible air:
From memory's lost beginning
Recollection from beyond time reminds that love
Is for nothing other;
But a state of being
                    long forgotten.

LIGHT OVER WATER

Brilliant
Myriad instantaneous alighting raindrops on a
    stream
That has run unbroken down and on
Since this once familiar place was home,
Each in its alighting flashes sun's glitter and is gone
As another, and another and another come to meet me,
Angel after angel after angel, its dancing-point
Always here and now,
The same bright innumerable company arriving,
Anew the present always absolving from time's flow.

Old, I know
How many, many, many the epiphanies of light.

And yet now as I write
They are only memories
Those bright arrivals of the travelling light,
Now nowhere, never again.
No road or bridge or gate
Into the past, once now, once here,
Nor farthest star comes near
Where they are gone, who once were dear;
For memory is Hades' house
Where none is present, where none meet.

And yet again, always
Those presences come to us, are seen, are known,
Messengers of meaning, sacred, indecipherable,
Present everywhere, to all.
Inaccessible as life their source;

We know untold, untaught
Who they are, what holy truth proclaim.
The knower a mystery, a mystery the known,
Forms of wisdom in perpetual epiphany, they and we,
Sun and eye, seer and seen,
Daily angels, sun and stars, river and rain.

Martindale, Nov. 27th 1983

MIMOSA-SPRAY

My dear mother
One mimosa-spray
Long ago, from an imagined Italy
She would never see
Offered her daughter
From a far-off blossoming tree.

Today
In a mimosa-grove
Heavy with flower-gold dust
I met in memory
My mother on that day
When I turned from her
Love's simplicity.

I who have rifled the world's beauty
Now will never enter
That golden garden she offered me.

A WINTER NIGHT

So tenuous and diffuse,
I no longer know myself
But through the momentary sense
Of what is present as I write–
Shadows of shadows, night, a candle-flame,
Closed shutters, and outside, the dark,
Lightning and rain.

Not arbitrary this or any here and now:
What is, product and due
Of a life lived hitherto,
Sum or minus of my days.
All means, is meaning,
Could I decipher what is given:
This the threshold where I stand
Without the key to enter the place I am.

I have much theoretical knowledge, can
Switch on or off some circuit of the brain,
Have written books on others' books of life,
But, deprived of words, am in the dark.
Tonight's lightning has put out
Our artificial light. A candle serves,
If not to read by, clear enough to pray.

I hear and fear
The destroyers of the storm,
Assailants of human houses,
Yet know their thunderous soundings
The music of the universe, immortal voices,
The choiring of the stars.
Hidden by storm and darkness the garden,
The sacred fountains.
I hear the waters running in their courses:
Flood-waters tell of cold, drowning, dissolving, flux,

Undoing, unbecoming,
Perhaps of freeing, though not
Of, but from, what I am.

Ninfa, Feb. 28th 1984

A SMALL matter
Whether I hope
To be blessed, or despair
With the lost, on the last
Or any day.

Enough to be
Part and particle
Of the whole
Wonder and scope
Of this glory.

Cannot even
The condemned rejoice
That the Presence
Is, and is just?

WORLD's music changes:
The spheres no longer sing to us
Those harmonies
That raised cathedral arches,
Walls of cities.

Soundings of chaos
Dislodge the keystone of our dreams,
Built high, laid low:
Hearing, we echo
Rumours of the abyss.

There was a time
To build those cloud-capped towers,
Imagined palaces, heavenly houses,
But a new age brings
A time to undo, to unknow.

TELL me, dark world,
What it is you know
That I dare not.

Destruction is the mode,
Love an old story
That none believes.

I ask the grass:
To every living cell
God's secret told,

Knowledge of the all,
In each seed
The axis mundi

Where blood is shed
Of one who dies
And rises from the dead.

I HAD meant to write a different poem,
But, pausing for a moment in my unweeded garden,
Noticed, all at once, paradise descending in the
    morning sun
Filtered through leaves,
Enlightening the meagre London ground, touching
    with green
Transparency the cells of life.
The blackbird hopped down, robin and sparrow came,
And the thrush, whose nest is hidden
Somewhere, it must be, among invading buildings
Whose walls close in,
But for the garden birds inexhaustible living waters
Fill a stone basin from a garden hose.

I think, it will soon be time
To return to the house, to the day's occupation,
But here, time neither comes nor goes.
The birds do not hurry away, their day
Neither begins nor ends.
Why can I not stay? Why leave
Here, where it is always,
And time leads only away
From this hidden ever-present simple place.

THE FORE-MOTHER

I AM spread wide, far
On the tide of the one sea,
As I ebb away
In lives not mine
My blood flows on.

Like a mist lifting
I fade,
I no longer am
Who through new eyes see
The green, the vein,
The flower, the tree.

I am an echo
You do not hear,
Who, gone from myself,
Am near
Your here and now
Of elsewhere.

I am long ago
Who am with you.
In your first love
Age-old, the untold
I speak to you.

LILY-OF-THE-VALLEY

No, it is not different,
Now I am old,
The meaning and promise
Of a fragrance that told
Of love to come
To the young and beautiful:
Still it tells
The unageing soul
All that heart desires
For ever is
Its own bliss.

THE PRESENCE

PRESENT, ever-present presence,
Never have you not been
Here and now in every now and here,
And still you bring
From your treasury of colour, of light,
Of scents, of notes, the evening blackbird's song,
How clear among the green and fragrant leaves,
As in childhood always new, anew.
My hand that writes is ageing, but I too
Repeat only and again
The one human song, from memory
Of a joy, a mode
Not I but the music knows
That forms, informs us, utters with our voices
Concord of heaven and earth, of high and low, who
     are
That music of the spheres Pythagoras heard.
I, living, utter as the blackbird
In ignorance of what it tells, the undying voice.

THREADING my way, devious in its weaving
  Into the web of the world,
Time's warp running from far back, and on
Of lives, crossed life-lines, intercrossed, entangled,
Knotted, knitted together, ravelled, unravelled,
Hidden, re-emerging in new design,
Always growing, unseen or seen
Patterns we make with one another, distant
Or near, from immemorial past
Into unbounded future running unbroken,
Threads so fine and subtle of lives
We weave and interweave, slender as light,
Intangible substance of the age-old
Ever-extending all, makers and made
Who feel the pull of love, of grief, on every thread.

WOODRUFF

TODAY the Presence
Has set before me
Woodruff's white foam
Of petals immaculate,
Fourfold stars numberless
Open life's centres,
In a London garden
They grow in a spring wood
Before the city and after
Machines whose noise
Tears the sky.
The white stars
Do not hear; they tell me
'The woods are always'.
Lily-of-the-valley
Feels for loam of leaves
And the blackbirds
Build anew, repair
The rents we tear
In times and places.
Immemorial woods
Are here, are near,
The white stars cross
The invisible frontier:
'Come to us', the flowers say,
'We will show you the way.'

SAY all is illusion,
Yet that nothing all
This inexhaustible
Treasury of seeming,
The blackbird singing,
The rain coming on,
The leaves green,
The rainbow appearing,
Reality or dream
What difference? I have seen.

WORLD, what have you done
With all those dear
Women and men
We have loved and known? Where
Are their voices, none
Like any other? Time,
Mysterious imperceptible flowing of now,
Where are they hidden? They were
Here, as we are, real
In the present, human and warm, familiar.
Where is the once, and how
Can we reach them there?

YES, it is present all, always—but these
Blind, ignorant, sealed senses shut me
From all I love, long for, know and am,
Weak moth fluttering against invisible pane,
Barrier not brick nor concrete, wood or iron,
Impenetrable because unknown.
Length of time endurance might outwait
Or world-wide space traverse,
Soar above height,
Drop by drop rain from heaven
Will wear away mountain, but where the way
Away from what I am, who, being this,
So faintly, briefly struggle in vain.

THAT flash of joy—
    Mine, or another's, or from elsewhere, far
Like scent of budding leaves borne on the wind,
Or pure note, clear,
Heart trembles to, like water in a glass,
Like a flame that bows and leaps
As sound-waves pass,
Poignant as first love remembered,
The past, the lost, the never-to-be
Glimpsed between the coming and the gone.
It seemed a room that I had lived in once
And found again just as it was,
But where that country out of time?
Was that recollection mine,
Or being itself, life in all its sweetness
Known for a moment, understood.

CHANGE

CHANGE
Said the sun to the moon,
You cannot stay

Change
Says moon to the waters,
All is flowing.

Change
Says the field to the grass,
Seed-time and harvest,
Chaff and grain.

You must change,
Said the worm to the bud,
Though not to a rose,

Petals fade
That wings may rise
Borne on the wind.

You are changing,
Said death to the maiden, your wan face
To memory, to beauty.

Are you ready to change?
Says thought to the heart, to let pass
All your lifelong

For the unknown, the unborn
In the alchemy
Of the world's dream?

You will change,
Say the stars to the sun,
Says night to the stars.

NAMED

I

In a dream, a voice
Called me by my name,
Unknown, or known from some far other time
Or place or state or world, yet nearer
Than here and now, that hidden one;
And was it I,
Unselved by sleep that takes away
All daily doing and being,
Absolved for a space from what we are, or seem,
Am I, who remember,
Another, or the same
Who stirred,
Who answered to my name
Recalled from lifelong years away, astray,
Forgetful and forgotten, since I had been
One named?
                  Strange among strangers my face,
Defaced, obscured, obliterate,
Falsified by the years, disguised,
Anonymous, who, when addressed,
Some other, or no-one;

Yet by that unknown knower I am known
And who I am.

II

But by what name
Did that voice summon?
The name my mother gave, not knowing
What child I was, who came
Into her house of life?
She gave me a name not mine
Who have so long forgotten
Who, what, whence, whither I am.

AN OLD STORY

I

I WAS in a garden
Where the trees flower,
Where birds sing
And waters run,

But my mind wandered
For a moment only
Of life-long time
I was astray,

A life-time gone—
But where are they,
The dazzling waters,
The creatures at play?

Still I see
White clouds, bright sun,
I touch young leaves,
Breathe the wild rose,

But they are far
As love from loss,
As come from gone.

II

This was not what I meant,
My life amiss

From day to day
How did I lose my way
From moment to moment?

The hours run on
Through the unkind act,
The lifelong loss,

But what is done
Long outlasts
Deed and doer,

There is no end,
From life to life
We repair what we can.

I have done what I am,
Am what I have done,
Yet meant far other.

III

Reader, I would tell
If I knew
That all shall be well,

All darkness gone,
All lives made whole,
Hearts healed that were broken,

Would tell of joy reborn,
Of wrongs made right,
Of harms forgiven,

But do not know
How what is done
Can ever not be,

Though love would wish it so.

IV

Who so well as the lost
Can know, from absence,
Who better, so far removed,
Measure by want love's fullness?
Of that kindness
In which a myriad creatures live in peace,
I, who know evil and good
Ask no mercy, yet
Claim as by right
Best right to praise.

BLUE COLUMBINES

For Jeremy

ALIGHT with dark
Fire, mystery
Kindled from seed to seed,
Garden to garden, spring to spring
Indigo
Darkness illuminate
Flaring at noon, colour of night-sky
Of the seven rays deepest
Solemnity of blue cathedral glory
Of womb, secret of shade,
Ablaze in my last garden, profound
Sounding of the afar, the beyond.

SEVEN SHORT POEMS

PARADISE—still I see
On autumn branches golden leaves
Cling to the blue sky
Just beyond, where I,
Though I remember, cannot be.

IN the November dawn
Of this world, I for a time
Seemed where the earth of dream
Was astir with the living roots of flowers to come.

PAPER-WHITE narcissi
Who were kind to me
Long ago,
You tell me now
That to the loveless
The dead send no messages
From neglected graves.

AGAIN the scent of lime
On the polluted air
Diffuses memories
Of a sweet far-off place
When we were there.

DOWNPOUR from thunder-cloud
Falling on cascade
Of white wall-roses,
Burnet-scented,
And in a swarm
Gnats are dancing
In the dancing rain.

FLIES—
But what I see
Flashing under leaves
As morning sunbeams fill the sycamore tree
Is flight
Of minute meteors, rays
In living transmutation of light.

THE WESTERN PATH

BRIGHT
Path over all waters,
Dazzling arrows, shards, sheets of brilliance
'More brilliant than a thousand suns'
From the first fiat reflected
From mirror to mirror
                          that light.

A RECKONING

WHAT do I know more
Than in my beginning,
Who, a child,

In innocence
Had done no wrong,
Had injured none,

Knew no remorse
To cloud the heart,
To darken the sun?

I through the years
Have toiled and striven,
My thought confused,

My heart seared
By memories
That beset the old,

Yet rich my days
In the world's wonders,
Flowers and birds,

Clouds and stars,
On northern hills
The curlew's cry,

Rich in knowledge
Of realms of thought,
Books that unfold

Visions and dreams
Of the human kingdom,
Temples and palaces,

Rich in the alone
Ever-presence
Of all that is,

In love and sorrow
That sound the heart,
All has been mine

Who must soon
Leave as I came
All I have been.

Was that child
I, who cry
'Never enough

'Of world's beauty,
'Faces of friends
'In rooms and houses

'Rich in kindness,
'Never enough,
'Of the inexhaustible

'Here and now
'Without end or beginning?'
The Presence replies

'What are you
'But one of the many
'Many-in-one,

'In the flow of time
'You have borne your share
'Of evil and good,

'Desire and despair,
'Hurting and healing,
'Of seeking and praying,

'Have carried the burden
'Of knowing and being,

'The irretrievable
'Unexpugnable
'Record of days.

'But the child unborn
'Is already the world's
'Flower and seed

'Of the wounding and weeping,
'The loss and the longing,
'The finding and seeking,

'For each is the all
'Of boundless being,

'Nor can the ending
'Of time unlive
'Life's myriad days,

'Unnumbered hours
'Of the numberless living,
'Music of heaven,

'Utterance of glory,
'The sound and the fury,
'The river of bliss.'

I listen and praise.

THE untold! My life all
I have not been or known
Of the rich perpetual
Flow that has carried me on
So far—far
From what bright star
The distance I have come,
Or gone, the distance still
To travel, whence we are:
Inaccessible to ourselves, our being.

FIVE POEMS

FRIENDS, who say
'You must write poems again',
What do you expect of me?
I have gone far away
From the springs and the streams,
The wild places
Now only names
Of memory: what remains?
Lamp, table, pen, hand
And the ever-presence
Only and always the same.

CAN I give comfort?
I know no more, reader,
Than you, in whose heart
Is the one life,
The one image imprinted,
Obliterate, defaced,
Forgotten, overlaid
By time, as in mine
Whom also love
Made infinite.

INTO what future do we pursue them
Who are already speeding
Into the past, with scarcely time to greet them
In the moment's meeting. We look beyond them
Into the never-to-be, where we seek them
Who are already gone, were with us only

In some unregarded here and now, the precinct.
In the unvalued present their sacred advent
Unheeded, yet made clear now we have lost them.

AT LAST the awaited opportunity, time free
Of all those tasks, imposed or self-imposed,
Yet now, trapped, I panic, try
To think of some pretext, anything to evade
A confrontation with the unwritten page.
There is no invisible visitant in my room:
The times and places are theirs, not ours,
Who make their presence present, infinite.
This blankness is the term
Of many evasions: we turn aside
Only for a moment into immeasurable absence.

HAND, pen
That must write truth,
Bitter world
That interposes darkness
Between remembered heaven
And shadowed earth,
The voice of joy
Sings on, but far away;
In sorrow's regions
I would bring comfort
With news of paradise, but memory
Of joy brings tears.

E VEN now, sky,
Sometimes I look up and say,
'No, I have not forgotten,
Though for the time
Going from here to there,
From this to next, I promise
(So I say to the blue spaces and high clouds)
To be again, someday,
In your great ever-presence'.
But silently you remind me always
That I have left, lost, gone away.

CHRISTMAS-TREE

For whom have I
As yet another year is ending
Decked this Christmas-tree
In blown-glass coloured balls and birds and shining
    spheres
And glitter on the ever-green
And living boughs? Who of the young
Who will come briefly to visit me
Will find magic in these tinsel stars, hear what they
    sing
Of memories not theirs, who must live on
Into years farther yet from Bethlehem?
No, not for the living,
It is my ghosts who will keep Christmas Past with me,
As it should be that an old woman
In all my remembered and unremembered presents be
With those who loved me, yet with whom, indifferent
    then,
Only now I am.

NATARAJA

I

TIME, rhythm
Of forms that open,
Forms that pass,

Perfect or marred,
The foot of the God
Is on the world,

Terrible dancer
Whose trampling tread
Crushes evil and good,

The flow of his river
Is in our blood,

End and beginning,
A beat of the heart
Our all, our nothing.

Destroyer of worlds,
The purifier,
His step indifferent,
His garment red.

II

How else
But by that trampling foot
Can be effaced
Our nightmare cities,
The dead-ends, the maze,
The culs-de-sacs,
The locked rooms, the windowless

Prisons, the closed minds,
The entrenched positions,
The safes, the cellars,
The death-proof shelters,
The high-rise towers of loneliness?

Who else
But the world-destroyer
Can free us from this state
And place of no return,
The inescapable consequence,
Impasse, end of the road.
We, fallen, can fall
No farther, hopes and fears
Converge in this
Term of what's done,
Thought, word and deed here end
In entropy. There is no-where to run.

I, who have become
What I am,
Am what I have done,
Free-will has come to this.
Back to the wall
I speak for all
Who, at bay,
Stand in extremis:
Only that Power can
Who will destroy us, free us.

Obliterate our trace, the fire,
The purifier!

NAMELESS ROSE

SOMETIME, some where
Always I hoped to find again
The rose whose trusses of pearl-
Shell-petalled flowers
Climbed to my first window-sill.
My mother did not know its name.

Some where, some time
That flourishing tree, whose buds, sun-warm
Opened gold-stemmed on the wall
Centres of sweet small roses
Whose petals fell too soon
I hoped to find,

But in no catalogue, no visited garden
My mother's nameless rose, until
Today in Italy, where summer
In multitude is blooming,
By a ruined wall I came
Upon a bower, and did not dare

To look too close, fearing to find
That rose too a stranger, yet
When I came near, each shell-pearl petal
Slipped into memory's place:
'Look, we are here', they told me, 'then
Is now again'. Almost

I believed them, for they were the same
As in those childhood summers past,
Those withered petals made anew;
But I was not, for years between,
Tears and estrangement, my mother's sorrow
No flowers could comfort, nor mine now.

Ninfa, May 13th 1986

WHAT of life?
Where my beginning,
Where my ending
Who am here and now
Hidden source
And ceaseless flow?
My room is small
Yet I am boundless,
The words I write
Others have spoken,
My heritage
Ancestral wisdom
From beyond time,
I speak again
To the unborn,
For being is endless.

What is death?
Where shall I go?
There is only here
And now is always.
Shall I remember
This life, this place?
What I have forgotten
Shall I know,
What I know
Shall I have forgotten?
Must I cease?
The music flows on.
Who then was I?
The eternal Presence
Moves through the grass.

THE INVISIBLE KINGDOM

WE know more than we know
Who see always the bewildering proliferating
Multiplicity of the common show.

There come to the artist's hands
Such subtleties of form, of light,
Gardens, presences,

Faces so tenderly beautiful
We wonder with what untaught knowledge seen,
Beyond the commonplace the hidden

Aspects of mystery, secrets
Known only to the soul,
Known only to love, immeasurable

Wisdom from our own hands' work grown,
Expression of a knowledge not our own
Which yet guides brush and pen, obedient

To an omniscience we, though ignorant, yet share
Whose hearts respond and answer
To Schubert's music, and Mozart's, they knowing no
        more

Than we of the celestial harmonies
They heard above the continual dissonance
The immediate imposes.

Yet unceasing
The music of the spheres, the magia of light,
Spirit's self-knowledge in its flow

Imaging continually the all
Of which each moment is the presence
Telling itself to the listener, the seer in the heart

Contemplates in time's river
The ever-changing never-changing face.

STORY'S END

O, I would tell soul's story to the end,
Psyche on bruised feet walking the hard ways,
The knives, the mountain of ice,
Seeking her beloved through all the world,
Remembering—until at last she knows
Only that long ago she set out to find—
But whom or in what place
No longer has a name.
So through life's long years she stumbles on
From habit enduring all. Clouds
Disintegrate in sky's emptiness.
She who once loved remembers only that once she
loved:
Is it I who wrote this?

WHAT human babe
Born in this world
Without a brimful cup
Of tears to weep—
But those tears shed
Dry-eyed
The heart weeps blood.

HONESTY

Too long astray—
Time, from hour to hour,
Lifelong, unending departure—

In my withering garden
A country flower,
'Honesty', prized for its signature,

Because, its seeds set,
Fall from a clear membrane,
Emblem of pure intent.

I thought to have come indoors
Not to this room
But to another, as it was,

Honesty and dried grass
In an alabaster vase,
Lamp alight, curtains drawn
Against the night—

Childhood, the holy day—
A moment, a turning away,
And never again.

H.G.A.

Too long away,
    You have drawn near, of late,
Or is it I,
Late, who return,
Nearing my end of time,
To your timeless place?
I have lived lifelong
My works and days with friends and strangers,
Now those ties
I and they have woven
No longer bind me, alone,
Duties, done or undone, forgotten.
How easily a lifetime falls away
And I stand free,
Now, again, as then.
Invisible companion ever young,
Lead me away
Where you will, beyond memories,
Beyond past days and vanished houses,
Remembered and forgotten faces.
Here is not my place, nor I this.

A DREAM

THOSE birds of dream,
    Circling high as eagles the skies of sleep,
Descending to rest in trees—
I saw with wonder birds of paradise,
Rainbow-hued, luminous
Their plumage, and others grey as doves.
Again into that inner sky they rose, but then
Returned once more to await. Are these
Birds of soul's country images
Of earth, remembered? Peacocks
Adorning miniatures of Brindavan, or Persian pages
Painted with two squirrel-hairs by craftsmen
Skilled in marvels,
Are they of inner or of outer skies,
Nature's splendour, or memory's?
Or are earth's peacocks' jewelled ocelli
Mirrors of paradise? Their plumes
That make the light shimmer are only dust
Of the earth, their lustre in the beholder's eye.
Where, of what land are they?
Or when did dust and spirit
So separate that creatures of clay
Ceased to mean heaven,
The birds of heaven fly from our waking world away?

HIDDEN

Today the curtain is down
The veil drawn over the face,
World only its aspect,
Tree, brick wall, dusty leaves

Of ivy, a bird
Shaken loose from the dust
It is the colour of. Nothing
Means or is.

Yet I saw once
The woven light of which all these are made
Otherwise than this. To have seen
Is to know always.

HAVE I not heard
Or only thought or hoped to hear
Those harmonies of heaven
That make the music of the world,

Waves of wind and tide,
Heartbeat and pulse
Of life, all songs,
All forms of being?

If they are there
With what dim vision
Looked daily on
Earth's holy face,

Yet if imagined only
Still the imaginable
Meaning and beauty
Of human thought,
Of heart's delight.

JESSIE

A COUSIN sent it me,
Found in the back of a drawer,
A broken brooch engraved with my mother's name,
Returned from long ago, when I
Knew by heart those silver clover-leaves and flowers
Small as forget-me-nots.
Then they were part of the known, whole world
My mother gave me; her name a message whose
      simple meaning
Is herself, once dear and familiar, now dear and far.

WHO ARE WE?

Not that I remember, but that I am
Memory, am all that has befallen
Unbroken being and knowing
Whose flow has brought me here, laden with the
    forgotten
Times and places, once here and now
Of those who were, from day to day,
From life to life, as I,
Presences of that omnipresence without end or
    beginning,
Omniscient through our being,
That brings and takes away the unremembered living
Moments of joy and wisdom, the once-familiar
Rooms and temples and fountains, the long-ago
    gardens
Of a thousand summers, music once heard,
Travelling through me and on, like a wave
Of sound, a gleam
Irrecapturable. And who are we
Who gather each one leaf, one life of the myriadfold
    tree
Of the lost domain, and mourn
The flowing away of all we never were, or knew?
Promises, messages reach us, instruct us,
The untold, the untellable, undying
Heart's desire, resonance
Of elsewhere, once, some day, for ever.

ALL SOULS

I, WHO in these shortening days
Am still in the company of the living
Who bear through time
All who were, are, or shall ever be,
Until the kingdom comes nor they or I shall see,
Who, from time immemorial sorrowing
Have heard the far-away music of immortal joy.

As this year darkens towards its close
I, until my last leaves fall,
Keep faith with that unending song
For those who were as now we are,
Remembering that imagined state and place
We never knew, nor they, that whence and whither
All come and all return.

In days to whose mornings we shall not wake,
To others we shall not know, that song will tell
That all is as the dead who in us will not rest
Would have it be, whose hearts beat on
In mine, through the October dark
Keeping the flame alight
Of all they never were, nor we.

Living I have traversed another day,
Kept faith still with what is not,
Has never been, that none has known
Who ever was, nor we
Whose memories are inexhaustible as time
Whom time can never satisfy,
That yet in time lives on in me.

A CANDLE FOR ALL SAINTS, ALL SOULS

For Antonia Klibansky

In this book, gift of an unknown friend
Hoping I might find words to kindle
Some illumination of mind or heart,
There remain many spacious pages where I still
May trace life's record, as the ant in dust,
The beetle under elm-bark, the snail
Its lustrous trail, or track of hare on the bare snow.
All leave their signature, as skeleton veins
Record spring's sap-flow in leaves once green.
What the pattern, what the meaning, these toilers
        know
Not more than I what or to whom I tell—
No more than the small house-fly that alights
Now on this page, whose script
Only the writer of the book of life can read.

On my shelves closed books of many lives,
Knowledge of the long dead, who lived these
        thoughts.
I have explored their regions of wisdom and wonder,
As others will relive their ever-present past
Whose records, written or unwritten, remembered or
        forgotten
Come to us in words spoken by living lips
Of the wise and the unwise, long-ago voices repeating
The never-ending stories of the loved and known
As being moves through every here and now,
        delighting
In all we have been and seen and done, endured,
Imagined and dreamed.

Fragments, traces remain, perfect like fossil shells,
Pages unfaded, painted walls, or sculptured stone,
Writings on bark or palm-leaves, scripts
Decipherable still by some, though few
Who from old manuscripts can rekindle the light
That once illumined texts of treasured wisdom
Transcribed by monks of Kells or Nalanda.
The gods themselves told the creation-stories
To those first ancestors whose scriptures were the
    stars
Who knew the speech of insect and bird, of rock and
    cloud,
The innumerable living, each a universe
Boundless in its own presence,
Undying in the imagination of the world.
I leave my trace, with theirs, in timelessness.

LONDON RAIN

THESE diamond spheres
Tainted from poisoned air that blows about the
  houses,
Each sour raindrop hanging from wire or railings
Yet catches its ray to open the rainbow light
Of heavenly promise before it falls
On sterile ground to moisten the patient moss
That mends with living green
Of Paradise, springing from blown dust in cracks and
  crevices
For lonely downcast eyes to find a long-ago familiar
  place.

LONDON WIND

WIND, lifting litter, paper, empty containers, grit,
Even here blows the element of air—
Between post-office and supermarket still the caress
Of earth's breath cool on my face
As gusts in spirals and eddies whirl
Spent leaves from London's plane-trees, to let fall
Perfect forms so lightly poised on a vandalized lot.

WISDOM OF WORDS

THROUGH this pen-point, this punctum
These old fingers inscribe my intricate line
Of words, beyond-price heritage from those
Who speak in soundless, loved, remembered voices
Of multitudes who in world's without-end times and
    places
Each in their once-and-for-ever here and now remains.

Sisters and brothers of dust, whose faces
I have never seen, young and beautiful, learned
Or wise, whose words have told
And tell me all your hearts have known,
Your long-ago loves are with me now and always
Who breathe the unbounded air that carries your far
    voices.

From word to word I trace my way, seeking, divining
Scarcely discernible messages, passing
From life to life clarities, marvels, epiphanies
All hearts, all souls have sought,
Bringing to my moment all those who once were,
    have dreamed,
Have known and praised, have sung, have cried aloud.

Cosmic music of water and wind and stars
Flows on for ever, but this human realm
Of meaning, none knows but we,
These memories, told and retold, imparted
From dream to dreamer by such as I,
Whose only knowledge is what we have made to be.

Sept. 8th 1987

BEFORE my eyes this page, my writing hand,
Books, lamp alight, fire low:
Shall I remember or forget
This time and place, my world
That none but I can know,
This secret, infinite here and now?

JOY

WHERE is joy, when?
I, being old, know
Joy here and now, always,
In every place, is in us
Who must die, must mourn,
Must soon be gone.

&

Joy, fragile, brief,
Soon, once, then, no-where—
But how beautiful, how clear
The sun, the light of life.

&

No need to tell of sorrow,
Of absence, loss—tears flow
From all eyes, offerings
To joy the heart remembers,
Whose lack all know.

&

Joy—
This morning against clear sky
Twigs of leafless sycamore
Gently stir
In the chill air

How far from joy—
Yet glad, because I
Myself who am the shadow
Before my eye
Must at last die.

FROM A GUEST-ROOM IN FIESOLE

As world speeds on,
I, in ever-present presence
Am always here and now,
My abiding-place life's day-to-day
Mornings and evenings, rooms, gardens, houses,
Where human faces come, and go.

In my old mind, the images
Of present and past presents merge and flow
Together, times and places of joys of sorrows,
Hopes, heartbreak, homecomings, partings, longings
    and dreams
As the ever-arriving, ever-departing world flows on
    and away.

Vistas of world's times and spaces open
Always before my eyes: that knot in the floor-board,
Those leaves of a walnut-tree
Outside this window, where below
Florence is a web of green and red and golden
    jewelled lights
Spread on the evening. Not Dante's Florence
Nor Beato Angelico's, nor Gozzoli's,
The city I see, but stranger to me
My own unknown unknowable than their past
As I traverse my life's uncharted realm
So briefly here, and never again, and anew.

PURIFY

PURIFY my sorrow,
Weeping rain,
Clouds that blow
Away over countries where none know
From whose heart world's tears flow.

Purify
My sorrow, bright beams
Of the sun's light that travels for ever away
From here and now, where I lie.

Purify
Heart's sorrow in the dust, in the grave
And furrow where the corn is sown,
End and beginning.

Purifier I cry
With the breath of the living,
Loud as despair, or low
As a sigh, voice
Of the air, of the winds
That sound for ever in the harmony of the stars.